Windshift

Windshift

Poems by

Barbara Loots

Kelsay Books

Cover Photograph: B.K. Loots
Author's Blog: www.barbaraloots.com

ISBN: 13-978-1-947465-46-6

Kelsay Books
Aldrich Press
www.kelsaybooks.com

In memory of Professor John S. Eells
who wrote on a college freshman's first essay
You have a talent for writing.

Acknowledgments

The author gratefully acknowledges publications in which some of these poems first appeared.

The Christian Century
Cricket
I-70 Review
Ladies' Home Journal
Landscapes With Women
Light Poetry Magazine
Lighten Up
The Lyric
Measure
Mezzo Cammin
Piedmont Literary Review
Potpourri
The Random House Treasury of Light Verse
South Coast Poetry Journal
Sparrow

The author gives wholehearted thanks to Tina Hacker for her keen editorial scrutiny and decades of friendship.

*Writing poems is not a career but a lifetime
of looking into, and listening to, how words see.*
—Philip Booth

Contents

I. Shoreline

II. Sunday School

III. Goose Sense

IV. In a Glass Darkly

About the Author

I. Shoreline

...O, but Everyone
Was a bird; and the song was wordless; the singing
will never be done.
—Siegfried Sassoon

The Healing

The world must love itself, the way it heals
over its wounds and gouges. It forgives
past injuries by starting something new.

Here on this island pioneered by you,
the ragged pines survive, the turtle lives
under the lily pads, the cedar kneels

at water's edge, not rooted in the stone
but leaning out until a winter storm
upended it. When we come back each year

we find few things just as we left them here.
We see the way new limbs and leaves transform
our views, old paths completely overgrown.

Windshift

We can be certain that the cold will come.
The monarchs moving south in ones and threes
begin their slow return where they came from
by instinct only, riding the August breeze
hundreds of miles. Mild as the evenings are
this year, the island teaches us the way
a sudden windshift from across the far
reaches of the lake can change the day
from soft to storm, from sun to rain,
and whip the flaccid sail out of control.
Some things we have no science to explain,
whether we drift or fix upon a goal.
We sit together, wordless on this rock,
breath and heartbeat rhythmic as a clock.

Relativity

Someone thought to mete out time,
how long it takes to pass.
So many drops from bowl to bowl.
So many grains through glass.

But time is merely here to there.
Sit still. Sit still and see
how time will disappear at once,
and you may simply be.

Entropy

What blaze of mind first learned to make a flame
from sparks and sticks, even before the word
had lit the fire of thought and kindled the name
of god and star, of animal and bird?

Fire, it said, for the upward-reaching tongue
of light held in one place for us to own
against all darkness, captive magic sprung
out of earth and sky, from sources yet unknown.

Confined indoors by pounding cold and rain,
we claim this foolish certainty of ours—
hearth and book, the small elements that remain
of mystery lost, gone worlds, and wasted powers.

Evening Elegy

The maples are the first to raise the flags
of autumn at the water's edge, their red
and orange and yellow show of motley rags
signaling colder, darker days ahead.
Beside them, gray veterans of past campaigns—
beheaded, pocked, naked, leaning—fall
slowly, roots softened by summer rains
and shoved downhill by the ineluctable
gravity of time, finally, into the lake.
Behind them, phalanxes of evergreen
stand fast as though no force could overtake
the young and strong. This peaceful evening scene
suspends for now the history of grief
that comes with burning log and turning leaf.

Shoreline

The birch's bony fingers make
     a final clutch at sun
before tree topples into lake,
     a brittle skeleton.

Cedars along high ledges lean
     their elbows on the boulder,
their heft of overhanging green
     pressed against its shoulder.

What unforgiving elements
     unearth them where they grow?
How long before the rock relents
     and shallow roots let go?

My narrow boat skims softly by,
     its dim reflection breaking
upon the water-mirrored sky
     a shiver of awaking—

this fragile shore our only heaven,
     a fringe of fern and flower,
whether the moment given
     be an eon or an hour.

Patterns

Be like the loon that wears
the pattern of the lake's ripples
on its back, that dives below
and swims upon and flies over
the water that is
its perfect home
and calls to its one mate
day and night
with three tones
Where are *you?*

Mysteriously Still

Sunlight dissolving
drips in the branches
spun through with silken
endeavor of spiders
shaping the air.

Uncertain rhythm of
sunlight dissolving
taps on the leaftips
plicking and plucking
the harps of white hair.

Strung among bushes,
hung from the pine trees,
sunlight dissolving
makes visible notes
for a numberless choir,

crescendo of insects
humming away
in the perilous thickness of
sunlight dissolving
the day to a blur,

where how many voices
stop at the heaven
of harp and of pearl,
mysteriously still in
sunlight dissolving.

Undone

Those thousands of Penelopes,
at night the spiders weave the trees
in clever-threaded tapestries

with filaments so finely spun
that at the touch of morning sun
their craftiness all comes undone.

Immense the tales we humans weave.
Yet faithfulness we may achieve
by learning what to unbelieve.

The Catch

To catch a poem, you must get a line
that's strong enough to hold a lot of weight
in case a thought, by luck or by design,

comes surging up, a shiver in your spine,
and strikes. Squirm of desire will be your bait
to lure the poem. Knot it on the line,

imagining the words that faintly shine
below the surface. Write the line, and wait
for luck or for the skill of your design

to work. A jerk! You summon all nine
Muses, astrophysics, hope, and fate
to hook the poem tugging on the line

unseen and powerful—perhaps divine!—
a thing that you yourself did not create
but knew it by the shadow of design.

You need an island and a jug of wine,
time, solitude, and books to contemplate
to fish a poem up. You get a line
and catch the thought determined by design.

Returning to the Island

These are the trees we hang the hammock on.
There is the spot where Billy caught a pike.
The hearth that your father fitted stone by stone.
The smoky old lamp your mother used to like.

Here are the chairs, no two of any kind.
The model boat with its musty sail half-mast.
All the old books, the toolbox left behind
to fix the neglect from summer seasons past.

Somewhere we'll find the coffee, matches, keys.
Everywhere, mice will show us where they've been.
Under no nearer, wiser stars than these,
everything dies, and something grows again.

Love Song

You are the butterfly whose wings
      stir up a rainfall in Peru.
The tropic fern unfurled that brings
      an earthquake in Tibet is you.

The cry bursting from blackbirds' throats
      that turns the tide on Iceland's shore
is you, and Sahara's dusty motes
      rosing the sunset in Lahore.

Who is the breath of an infant's sigh
      that sparks the heart of a unicorn?
The rock streaking the moonless sky
      that wafts a feather around Cape Horn?

You, the invisible silver thread
      between Zanzibar and Amsterdam.
Even by thought unlimited,
      whatever the you may be, I am.

II. Sunday School

God never seems to weary of trying to get himself across.
...When the Creation itself doesn't seem to say it right—
sun, moon, stars, all of it—he tries flesh and blood.
—Frederick Buechner

Rachel

The wind howls down the Haran hills tonight
and fills the camp with moans and whispering.
The feast is done, and in the bridal tent,
my bulbous sister, full of fear and wine,
dark-veiled and silent as befits a bride
deceives the husband who was nearly mine.
I lie awake imagining his arms
heaving her body like the lifeless skin
of water that he once poured out for me.
It almost makes me laugh.
                            My woman's task,
lifting the dripping skins out of the depths
to succor dull-eyed sheep and listless dogs,
gave me no joy until the day he came
these seven years ago, and turned the stone,
and drew the water from my father's well.
He kissed me, and he wept. From that day on,
I lived to be the woman that he loved.

My clever father never mastered him
although they bargained like a pair of thieves.
Until tonight.
                Are Laban's daughters sheep
that stand with equal purpose for the ram?
This trick will be uncovered by the sun.
Its consequences cannot be undone.
His shepherd's hands, as soft as they are strong,
entangle even now in Leah's hair.
The eager bridegroom slow to realize
how cold her blood is, and how slack her thighs,
will get the son that would be ours in her,
and murmur *Rachel, Rachel* in his sleep,
while bartered and beloved rage and weep.

Abigail

I care for him although he is a fool.
But when old Nabal turned the king away
and felt so smug, I nearly blew my cool.
I had to act, or there'd be hell to pay.
I packed the wine, the raisins, and the bread,
some sheep prepared for roasting and some grain,
and sent the young men with the mules ahead
in secret. Nabal hasn't got a brain
for politics. He can't help feeling proud
of what he owns. I am this rich man's wife.
I'd rather bear his child than weave his shroud.
So I'll go plead with David for his life.
I'll reason with the sot when I get back.
But my guess is, he'll have a heart attack.

Michal

Michal leaning out her window
watched David leaping and dancing
before the Lord.

To be jealous of God
whips the heart
cold as wind over a lone rock
at night in the desert.

For she wanted him
all to herself, this king,
no happier in his nakedness
than her body could make him,
never to leap except
in her exaltation,
nor to have joy beyond the house
of her father.

And this woman who loved
what was next to God
but not God
departed alone to her room
and wept in anger
until she was old.

Bathsheba

I knew beforehand how he used to pace
the parapet by moonlight
thinking of his shepherd nights on the precipice

where he watched over helpless ewe and lamb
like he looked down on me. Naked, I might entice
this king, as hot as any rutting ram,

to yearn for yet another concubine,
and, playing the innocent, the undefiled,
I might devise to make his pleasure mine.

At first, I did not hope to move
his heart. Escape alone was my design.
I weighed no consequence of love.

My time draws near. I fear this morbid child
that waxes great in me. What horrid figures make
its limbs thrash like the throes of the wild

warrior dying in his tackle for the sake
of my ambition? Night after night,
a terror in the stars keeps me awake.

Susanna in the Spa

Sending a cloud of steam up
over the rooftop, Susanna
lifts the lid of the spa,
shucks her terrycloth robe,
slips in and slides down.

Stars angling upward revolve
over the backyard fence
recycling ancient stories
as she tilts her head back
into the hot pool.

Down from a dark window
one old neighbor ogles her
breasts that float like moons,
two moons among the stars
on the still water.

A dog barks. A car rattles
by. A siren somewhere sets out
in blue pursuit. A meteor slices
between Taurus and Orion.
Susanna looks up.

Noah's Wife

I am waiting in the middle of all this land
for the ocean to come
to me. Here, sunflowers leaning down.
Under the dust, gray faces. Their shadows
standing still. I am waiting
beside my house for signs of rain,
having done
everything I can. My house
harbored in the grass, or rather
beached. An abandoned life. Far
off on the dun sky scum-loaves
sludge together. Some
promise. I am warning you
how nothing can be saved by itself.

When the Water Went Down

When the water went down, old Noah
was left with a world to tend,
the same wild seed to nurture,
the same ploughshares to mend,
the same chores every morning,
the same wife in his bed,
the same unanswered longing,
the same desire and dread—
but no one to shake his fist at,
no secret cause to gloat.
And Noah yearned for a reason
to build him another boat.

A Cat Recalls the Exodus

For the Lord commanded Moses concerning the cats
at the departure of the Children of Israel from Egypt.
—Christopher Smart, "Jubilate Agno"

The book of Moses never mentions cats,
although he might have thought our power divine
who saved his people from the plague of rats
you never heard of, thanks to me and mine.
When Egypt let them go, along we went
on backs of beasts with sacks of gold and grain.
We'd make ourselves at home in any tent,
and listen to that ragged mob complain
until old Moses nearly had a fit.
But we were grateful for the feast of quail
that fell each evening. We cats loved to sit
with Moses while he spun tale after tale
of people whining, like at Rephidim.*
Yet not a word of how we stuck by him.

*Exodus 17: 1-7

Cat

To make an idol
I would devise
a fistful of daggers,
Byzantine eyes,
clever machinery
covered in fur,
eloquent posture,
inscrutable purr.

The Old Soldier Speaks

I took the money. But with my last breath,
I tell you, I am not afraid of death
because of what came over me that day.
An earthquake rocked that blasted stone away
and lightning struck us blind.
                    The corpse was gone.
Some women came and found us, close to dawn,
two simple soldiers up against the wall,
about to cut our throats and end it all
before the charge of dereliction fell.
So what would you have done?
                    We ran like hell.
Of course, they found us, then cooked up a lie
to spread around, and bought our alibi.
Years later, I still dream about that night—
the heaving ground, the terrifying light.
But from the start, no matter what I said,
                    I knew that Galilean wasn't dead.

Brother Martin

Awake all night in a cold sweat of prayer,
he hears the devils writhing underneath
his bed. In the shut cell, their sickening breath
prickles his nostrils with the foulest air.
What must he suffer never to be pure?
What punishment of everlasting death
shall he deserve for merely being Luther?
What anguish and uncertainty endure
who cannot find a goodness nearer God's,
and would not buy the way to paradise?
Brained by lightning, marching as to war,
at last he stakes his life on holy odds,
takes the stone steps, a pirouette of grace,
and nails his mighty doubts on heaven's door.

Caterpillar

In perfect proclamation
that piety will do
it shrugged its fur,
it shed its house,
it fasted
and it flew.

Natural History

We bow continually to the gods
that press down on us heavily as stones.
Contentious spirits cause our burning hands
to carve out sockets for their eyes,
to make them wings of wood,
to set their teeth in bones.
Their voices moan among us
like wind in the mouths of caves.
O multifarious father, these children believe all things,
in each begetting make your image new.
Each generation shoulders up a shaft
against the weight, against the weight of you.

Magdalen

Even our sensuality has nothing but mind to reside in.
—John Frederick Nims

Magdalen of words, I'd curl up in any mind
that welcomed me. Kissing a stranger's feet
while he stroked my hair, I'd find
whatever he said to me terrible, and sweet.
I'd pour out as well my fragrant tale:
love's adventures drip between my hands
holding this fine and fragile grail.
Comes there a man who understands,
let alone answers, my ambiguous need?
I'd let him touch me. No, teach me
          to hear, to read.

III. Goose Sense

Laugh and the world laughs with you...

—Ella Wheeler Wilcox

Care to Reconsider?

René Descartes drops by a bar
To quaff a couple beers.
The barkeep says, "You want a shot?"
René Descartes says, "I think not."
And POOF! He disappears.

At Fifty

At fifty, most of life is maintenance.
You own too much, and what you own owns you.
Day-to-day's a frantic little dance
And keeping up is all there's time to do.
Forget the pile of books you haven't read—
more books are being written every day.
That weekend hour you'd like to spend in bed?
Well, sleep is too much with us anyway.
You thought by now you would have earned enough
to concentrate on art, improve your soul.
But life is eaten up by all your stuff,
and getting out of debt is still a goal.
Since when did coffee breaks become a crime?
And writing sonnets just a waste of time?

Goose Sense

The Canada geese on their morning commute
from the north to the south of the lake
are the crankiest crowd on the aerial route.
What hubbub of honking they make.

I'll hear, as the evening puts on its display,
the same gaggle of geese going forth,
ending their day in the noisiest way
as they flap from the south to the north.

The north and the south and the east and the west
look alike to my innocent eye.
This daily commotion may be for the best.
But only a goose would know why.

My Cat Has a Number of Places

My cat has a number of places she sits in.
The sliver of chair where my derrière fits in.
The top of the pillow when my head is on it.
The paper on which I am writing a sonnet.
The tread on the stairs where my step is unsteady.
The jacket laid out when I've brushed it already.
The book in my lap that I'm keen to get through with.
Between me and someone I'm wanting to woo with.
The page of the *Times* that I'm reading the news on.
The shelf in the closet I'd like to put shoes on.
Way under the bed where no arm's reach can get her
when anyone kind wants to meet her or pet her.
The arm of the sofa I'd like to recline on.
The place at the table I'm fixing to dine on.
In front of the sink when I'm washing the dishes.
The spot she's *not wanted's* the one that she wishes!

Brother Dog Sister Cat

Dog is dumber than a TV husband,
Trusting as a cuckold in a Shakespeare play,
Faithful as a 19th century butler,
Sentimental as a drunk on New Year's Day.

Cat is cagey as a fortune teller,
Loopy as a starlet in a 1930's role,
Sensuous as smoke around a stripper,
Elusive as conviction in the soul.

A collaborative poem. First stanza written by Gail White.

Colonoscopy: A Love Poem

My love is like a red, red rose.
I know because I've seen
the photographs inside of him
projected on a screen:

the petal-like appearance of
his proximal transverse,
his mid-ascending colon
like a rose's opening purse,

appendiceal orifice,
a bud not yet unfurled—
Oh, what a pleasing garden is
my true love's inner world!

How very like a red, red rose
his clean and healthy gut.
I love my laddie all the more
since looking up his butt.

"Donor" Nobis Pacem

I've shed more blood than Jesus.
There's really nothing to it.
From time to time, I've saved a soul
and didn't die to do it.

I haven't got a golden crown
for gallons I have given,
no promise of eternal life,
no glory ride to heaven,

no mystic explanation,
no complicated creed.
A bag of hemoglobin
fulfills the human need.

O beautiful the bleeding heart,
O-negative the way
that leads to the salvation
of someone's child today.

My body manufactures cells
that oxidize like rust.
O Lord replenish them, I pray,
until I turn to dust.

Her Former Fat Self Speaks

The clothes she's wearing now are hers, not mine.
But nothing's bagged up for the DAV.
She's practical. I take that as a sign
that she's a long way from forgetting me.
God knows I put up a terrific fight
against the slow erosion I endured
for months, while she observed me day and night,
the history between us oddly blurred.
The image she admires is youthful, svelte.
She claimed to love the loveliness within,
but more when solid flesh began to melt,
as though our very nature made us sin.
I'm gone. For now. There's nothing to forgive.
But we both know she has to eat to live.

Clearance

You love these red ones with the four-inch heel.
Just take them down and try them on for size.
Whoa! Wouldn't *those* enhance your sex appeal!

And at a closeout price. Boy—what a steal!
But wait a minute. Wonder if it's wise
to take the risk. Red shoes? A four-inch heel?

When you consider they could make you feel
unsteady as a drunk, you'd compromise
your safety. And for what? Your sex appeal?

A broken ankle is a bad ordeal
at your age, girl. And still you fantasize
risqué potential in a four-inch heel?

You think a shoe will do the trick? Get real.
Your dancing days are done with darling guys
attracted by your brains and sex appeal.

Except they weren't. Youth wasn't that ideal.
You can amuse yourself with harmless lies.
But don't forget the creep. The clod. The heel.
You know there's more to life than sex appeal.

The Aisle Not Taken

Two aisles diverged in a CVS,
And sorry I had to stop and guess,
A lonesome shopper, long I stood
And looked down one as far as I could
To where it appeared I'd find success,

Then took the other, as straight a line,
And having perhaps the better claim
Because it displayed a likely sign;
Though as for that, these eyes of mine
Could scarcely discern a product name.

On shelf after shelf the boxes lay
With every size and every brand
In a vast and colorful array.
Oh! How could I make a choice that day?
My brain cells failed to understand.

I shall be telling this with a sigh
Sometime many a headache hence;
Two aisles diverged—bumfuzzled, I—
I took the one to Exit by
And fled from the place in self-defense.

Dragging the Main

They do it still, in early June
on Friday night in Hannibal.
The ritual: dragging the main
to roar their summer mating call.

The male whose license plate is lit
with purple neon makes each pass
conspicuous in plumage that
conveys the signal *Senior Class.*

It's June. And soon the tourist swarm
will set the local lads and lasses
out of neighborhood and farm
to selling tickets, filling glasses,

but tonight, the street is packed
and loud with lurid shouts of love
from car to curb. The cops stand back
and only mildly disapprove.

The Romance

A three-legged person is living upstairs.
I know it because of the socks that he wears
that emerge from the dryer in trios not pairs.

He has a companion who seems to make do
with only one sock. So perhaps it is true
that she manages nicely with one foot too few.

They met in the laundry and hit it off great,
this three-legged man and his one-footed mate
in a perfectly heartwarming cycle of fate.

Antisocial Network

Forgive me, but I will not be your friend
on Facebook. Even though you somehow found me,
I've clicked Ignore. I'm sorry. That's the end.

I'm firm in this refusal to extend
the circle of acquaintances around me.
Forgive me that I will not be your friend.

I understand the gesture you intend,
and yet however lightly or profoundly
our lives have intersected, I must end

things here before eternal ripples blend
our separate histories on common ground. We
are not related. You are not my friend.

Your photos, the opinions you defend,
your escapades and preferences astound me.
Who *are* you anyway? This has to end.

I'm certain nothing vital will depend
on simply multiplying how renowned we
think we are. The friend of every friend
is not my friend. That's you. And that's the end.

IV. In a Glass Darkly

For now we see through a glass, darkly; but then face to face: now I know in part; but then shall I know even as also I am known.

—I Corinthians 13: 12   King James Version

What Is

Cosmology is really just theology for people who can do math.
                                        —Unknown

Most of the universe, say scientists,
is undetectable, a force so vast
that planets, stars, all matter rushing past
our eyes and instruments, cannot resist,
and even light is now regarded less
as the eternal boundary of time.

Who is to say which art is more sublime?
Astronomers and theologians guess
the origin of earth, of humankind,
whether of God or mathematics made—
for both, the thought of what is undisplayed
a dark, compelling suction in the mind.

Winnowing

How hard it is to winnow the dreams from waking,
To watch the gold illusion drift away
And turning to the delicate grain of morning
Grind it into the plain bread of day.

Irony

You women who grew up with wash and wear
have no idea what your grandmas knew
of steamy love. Before this easy care,

they ironed out their longing and despair
from baskets filled with more and more to do
as little girls grew up well-washed, to wear

no evidence of wrinkles anywhere.
They smoothed away the daily residue
with steamy love, hard work, uneasy care.

The padded board became an altar where
they wept and sang, believing it was true
that women must grow up to wash, and wear

their hearts on others' sleeves. They pressed their prayer
in pillowcase and collar, breathing through
their steamy love with never-easy care.

I think of how they labored to prepare
a better life for daughters to pursue,
for women who grew up with wash and wear
and steamy love that ends in easy care.

Costumes

The pleasure lies in putting costumes on,
and not in caring if the play is real.
You can adjust the serious face for fun
and wink behind the mask of how you feel.
Imagination poured from a carafe
transforms the colored water into wine.
A bit of business here will make them laugh.
You change ambitions with a clever line.
Another day, you play another part
and leave last summer's image on the shelf.
While others praise or criticize the art
you put on age as though it were yourself
then when you're done, unhook it at the chin
and shrug the sweaty thing into a bin.

Taking Up Ballet

I've learned that how they move is never free.
Those slaves to dance, their weightless moments bought
with pain, perform each arc to its degree,
perfected by intensity of thought.
These lessons burst my bubble of romance
and teach me more than how to point my toe.
Some say if you must count it isn't dance.
But counting is the only part I know.
I am too old for this. My knees protest.
I sweat. I stink. I stumble at the barre.
Not altogether hopeless, but depressed,
I comprehend the way things really are,
yet strive to dance. In my imaginings,
I see Nijinsky smiling in the wings.

Retirement

The day after the send-off of her friends
and colleagues after almost forty years,
the weight of freedom instantly descends.

She tweaks the puzzled cat behind the ears
and pours herself more coffee. Still undressed
at ten o'clock, she feels the grind of gears

against the drag of useless time. The rest
of Wednesday is eternity to her,
the old routine undone, the new unguessed.

She hears, from blocks away, the muffled purr
of cars and trucks that have somewhere to go.
She gazes at the empty calendar.

She was, as Human Resource records show,
dependable, a model employee.
New hires could always count on her to know

procedures. She would rarely disagree
with bosses, though it happens, when it came
to better job or bigger salary,

that no one influential knew her name.
And so the work she did so well remained,
from start to finish, pretty much the same.

You'll be secure, the counselor explained,
with years of income from an IRA
and interest that your prudent saving gained.

The antique clock they gave her chimes its way
toward noon. It's raining. Summer thunder booms.
She wonders what to fix for lunch today.

The carefree life she never longed for looms.
She'll never finish picking up her rooms.

Just Make the Coffee

for Jodi

You have to get over it, being a woman and all,
that history turns on the sayings and doings of men.
The tears and the trials of women, we cannot recall.
The trail of her story will never be traveled again.

Even the Marys were speechless for most of the book.
Mother and friend and the lover anointing his head
had little to say. But consider the courage it took,
giving birth, being loyal, reporting the words of the dead.

We just have to be there, intelligent, practical, mute,
while men with their pencils are busily spinning the tale.
But dogma and ritual, bluster and bloody dispute
will not—over listening and touching and loving—prevail.

In a Dry Season

All summer the sun has eyed this wounded ground
lying cracked under the stubble. The round
earth, like a huge pot pieced together
by each generation's guesswork, wants new weather.

Murmurs from the limp leaves and the furled grass
pleasure the clouds that lean down when they pass,
until at last rain mutters over the field
its prayer that every brokenness be healed.

Pedestrian Beware

for Tina

Pedestrian beware in Amsterdam.
The cyclists never stop. They'll mow you down.
Or you can get run over by a tram.

A tourist failed to look around, and BAM!
It was an accident of low renown.
Pedestrian beware in Amsterdam.

Deleted quick as pornographic spam,
a widow on a late-life fling in town
on Leidsestraat was flattened by a tram.

A couple on a cruise from Birmingham
were shipped back home with many a solemn frown.
Pedestrian beware in Amsterdam.

One minute you're as happy as a clam.
The next you miss a step and crack your crown
and take your last look upwards at a tram.

A speeding Vespa hits you with a slam
that hurls you in a near canal to drown.
Pedestrian beware in Amsterdam.
A bike will wipe you out, if not a tram.

Tulip Mania

*In the winter of 1636-37, a valuable bulb could
change hands ten times a day in Amsterdam.*

What elemental hunger grips
        the hearts of those who know
the promise of unfurling lips
        from that dark bulb below.

Mysterious swirls of amethyst
        and scarlet tongues of fire
engorge the narrow garden kissed
        by winter's cold desire.

What crowded caravansaries
        the gathered globes suggest
whose silken frills and filigrees
        unfold to be caressed.

Embrace the momentary power,
        sell everything you own,
possess the pearl, the perfect flower
        that blooms for you alone.

At Angkor Thom

Learn what you can from what they left behind,
the great stone faces smiling and serene,
their voices silent and their stone eyes blind.

Consider how these towers were designed
to speak of powers in a world unseen
turned into images they left behind,

the features of a paradise aligned
foursquare, and walls that scene by scene
tell stories of the past: embattled, blind

warriors, fishing, feasts, the daily grind
twelve hundred years ago. The green
lichen eats the stones they left behind.

These terraces reveal the mastermind
of engineers and artisans whose keen
directives came from gods whose eyes are blind.

Now from our hands the furls of incense find
a path to heaven. Tell us what you mean
to say in stone on stone you left behind.
Your voice is silent, and our eyes are blind.

Memoir

Like an old purse discovered in a drawer,
the heart spills out detritus from the past—
the fume of memory in the scent you wore,
clues to a beauty never meant to last.

The stub of youth a half-forgotten play.
The key to wishes closed behind you now.
The scribbled numbers of a certain day
you took a chance perhaps, or broke a vow.

A mirror shows how rude the years have been.
How crumpled is the stuff you've kept so far.
How darkly loves and dreams endure within.
How carelessly abandoned some things are.

Checking Out

A slip of paper underneath the door
with all the charges listed is your cue:
today is checkout time. You know the score.
Your stay is up. The black car comes for you.

You jam a kind of suitcase with the stuff
picked up while you were here, but sadly find
there isn't world or time or space enough.
You have to leave your whole damn life behind.

Obituary

So she is dead before we even thought
that she was sick. She chose. The cancer grew
with no "courageous battle" ever fought,
no patronage, no probing interview,
no Facebook page promoting prayer for her,
no million dollar drugs, no telethon,
no foreign clinic promising a cure,
no holding out for hope. She's simply gone.

I want to be as definite as that
when my turn comes, ineffably to keep
my final secret like a Cheshire cat,
serenely smiling as I fall asleep.

I wish I would have been there at her side
to say, You go, Girl! just before she died.

Tornado

Suddenly a monster puzzle has been dumped
across the landscape where a town had been.
Stunned, they wonder, *How do we begin?*
Utterly stumped.

A hunk of wall. A wheel. A shred of tree.
A gas pump up against a kitchen stool.
A mound of colors. Could there be a school
in that debris?

The neighborhoods designed in tidy blocks
must be assembled, jumbled gardens swept
up, broken pieces found and kept
in a small box.

They pick among the rubble for some clue
buried in the odd shapes they lift and shove
around, trying to reconstruct the picture of
things they once knew.

Hundred Year Flood Releases Old Pioneers

Newspapers report a large number of unearthed coffins float miles away

Drifting oarless over the drowned farms
where broken levees let the river sprawl

the wheel-less wagons never touch the road,
avoid the dusty taste of traffic jams.

Away from wires and lives that crowd too near,
they move again along an unmarked trail.

We'll round them up, try to discover names,
shovel them under in a place that's dry,

until a hundred years from now they hear
the rumble of axles in the lowering sky.

In a Glass Darkly

Glass Labyrinth Robert Morris 2013
The Nelson-Atkins Museum of Art,
Kansas City, Missouri

*This sculpture is a true labyrinth with
one single path.* —Curator's Note

Transparent parable has come to pass:
whoever walks this labyrinth of glass
will soon discover how the turns deceive
what eyes can see and make the mind believe.
For here and there, you note a bloody smear
where someone's nose learned suddenly to fear
the impact of assumption and of haste,
the painful price of confidence misplaced.
Slow down. Slow down. Do not presume to know
there's clarity in where you have to go.
The path ahead, a triad corridor.
The ground beneath, a narrow, crisscross floor.
A frieze of greasy groping on the wall.
No guidance seems reliable at all,
for out of reach, before you and behind,
the travelers in all directions wind.
But let your single purpose be about
the work of going in and getting out.

About the Author

Hundreds of verses into her career as a writer for Hallmark Cards, Barbara Loots remained essentially anonymous. However, her optimistic view of life touched thousands of lives with a broad swath of social communications, from birthdays to holidays to care of the grieving. She is the author of a number of children's books published by Hallmark, including *Fun on the Farm With Numbers*, now in the Smithsonian collection of pop-up books.

Her work as a poet has been appearing since the 1960s in magazines such as *The Lyric, Blue Unicorn, New Letters, Measure, Cricket,* and *The Christian Century.* Anthologies include *The Random House Treasury of Light Verse, The Random House Book of Poetry for Children, The Helicon Nine Reader, The Muse Strikes Back, The Whirlybird Anthology of Kansas City Writers,* and *Landscapes With Women.* Online, her poems can be found at *Mezzo Cammin* and *Light Poetry Magazine.* Her chapbooks are *The Bride's Mirror Speaks* and *Sibyl & Sphinx* (with Gail White). Her collection *Road Trip* was published by Kelsay Books / White Violet Press in 2014.

In the formalist tradition, she writes with admiration for such poets as Robert Frost, Richard Wilbur, Edna St. Vincent Millay, and Gerard Manley Hopkins. She resides in Kansas City, Missouri, where she volunteers as a Docent for the renowned Nelson-Atkins Museum of Art, and worships with the Presbyterians at Second Church. She is married to Bill Dickinson and obeys orders from Bob the Cat.